THE BRADFORD POISONING OF 1858

THE BRADFORD POISONING OF 1858

GEORGE SHEERAN

Ryburn Publishing

First published in 1992
Ryburn Publishing Ltd
Krumlin, Halifax

© George Sheeran
All rights reserved
No part of this publication may be reproduced, stored in a retrieval system, or transmitted in any form or by any means without the prior permission of the publisher and copyright owner except for the quotation of brief passages by reviewers for the public press

ISBN 1 85331 033 6

Composed by Ryburn Publishing Services
Origination by Ryburn Reprographics

Printed by Ryburn Book Production, Halifax, England

Contents

1	SETTING THE SCENE	7
2	THE FATAL EVENTS	13
	The Error	13
	The Mixing	14
	The Marketing	14
	A Lesson on Poisons	17
	Mr Leveratt Takes Charge	17
	Counting the Cost	20
3	THE PRISONER AT THE BAR	23
	Remanded	23
	Mr Baron Watson Considers	24
4	LATER YEARS	27
	Dramatis Personae	27
	In the Public Interest	30

1

Setting the Scene

The terrible events of 1858 took place in a Bradford which has vanished. Scarcely a trace remains. The Victorian Bradford we know today is one which we have in common only with the generations born after 1880.

> ... so great a transformation has taken place and the old so completely given way to the new that anyone revisiting Bradford after an absence of a quarter of a century or so, would fail to recognise it ...

William Scruton, a Bradford historian, wrote that in 1889, for even then older parts of the town were being cleared away to make room for the new. So it's important to get to know something of Bradford as it stood in the 1850s.

Before 1800 Bradford did not rank alongside such important places as Leeds or Halifax. It was a substantial Yorkshire market town, where people also made worsted cloth, and that's the way things were until the 19th century. But soon after 1800 the position began to change as the market town grew into an industrial district of importance. In 1801 its population had been 6,393; but by 1851 it had risen above eight times to 52,493, making it the second most heavily populated town in the area after Leeds.

People poured into Bradford from the outlying districts to take up employment in the increasing numbers of textile mills, factories and workshops, or to find jobs in the construction industry, or set up in business as small shopkeepers or craftworkers. The birth rate was high, and the population was added to further by a stream of immigrants from Ireland.

By 1850 the town centre was a muddle of factories, houses and small shops with many pubs in between. The majority of the fine public and commercial buildings that we know today had not been built then – there was no Town Hall or Wool Exchange, and St George's Hall was begun only in 1851. True, along Piccadilly some better quality architecture had begun to appear in the form of wool warehouses of the 1830s and here too was the old Exchange whose massive portal survives today near to the junction of Piccadilly and Kirkgate. There was also the new Court House, a handsome building, erected on Hall Ings in 1834. But this was all that Bradford had to offer. For the most part it was a grim and smoky factory town.

Bradford from the north, a view of perhaps the 1860s.

Smoke characterised Bradford as far as Georg Weerth was concerned. Weerth was a German working in Bradford in the 1840s, and although he knew other industrial towns – Manchester, Leeds, Birmingham – Bradford, he felt, was the worst, as "if I had been taken straight to Hell." The chimneys of its many factories made life intolerable –

> In November and December ... perpetual darkness lies, for the most part, over the town; it is like living at the North Pole in week-long obscurity; in thick coats, mouths and nose tied up with scarves, the people creep like ghosts through the mist and smoke, whose gloomy clouds have settled in charming union upon the alleyways.
> [*The Writings of George Weerth*, translated by Alan Farmer, Bradford Central Library]

To escape the smoke, those who could afford it made their homes outside the town. Already suburbs were emerging at Little Horton and Manningham. Wealthy manufacturers were building houses at the north end of Manningham and around the pleasant fields of Girlington. Others lived in houses nearer to the town along Manningham Lane and Manor Row. Manufacturers, merchants, the professions together with clerks and tradesmen all had houses here, and around Southfield Square and Lumb Lane.

But where Lumb Lane joined Westgate, here the dividing line between the respectable and the disreputable was drawn. Across Westgate the land

Goitside, a view of the 1880s.

falls away down towards Thornton Road and the centre of the town. In the 19th century this was a mass of back-to-back cottages, workshops, lodging houses, courts, alleyways, old tenemented buildings, beerhouses and down-at-heal corner shops. Longlands, the Leys, Goitside – these were districts where no respectable person ventured, and things were to remain that way for another thirty years and more. As James Burnley, a Bradford journalist of the day, observed, "it behoves one to tread gingerly, and to be cautious in one's utterances in order to avoid a broken head."*
The area around Longlands was Bradford's Irish quarter, a place where "squalor, filth, and darkness seem to reach the culminating point of disgrace", and where the same journalist was shocked by the raggedness of the children and the lack of home comforts.

* This and the following quotes are taken from James Burnley's *Phases of Bradford Life.*

The Parish Church looking towards the town. To the right we see a cluster of ramshackle housing around Church Steps and the bottom of Bolton Road.

But squalor and poverty were not confined to the Irish. Bradford's web of slums spread across the congested centre of the town and reached along Wakefield, Manchester and Leeds Roads; along Church Bank towards North Wing; and along Bolton Road to Wapping. The town end of Bolton Road was becoming the haunt of prostitutes, as Burnley was to describe in his investigations into Bradford's night life. His disgust was aroused there on seeing "a young gaily attired, brazen-tongued female, walking up the road with a well-dressed young man on each side of her". Later he was to spy "the three votaries of vice", making merry in an oyster shop.

Of course, it would be quite wrong to give the impression that everyone who lived in the areas mentioned were ignorant, criminally minded or bent on vice. Many decent working families lived there, also. But undoubtedly the network of streets and courts which spread up and out of central Bradford was a desperate place to live.

During the day these districts were comparatively quiet. Nights were a different question. Nowadays we are getting used to the idea of shops being open later in the evenings. Victorian Bradford was ahead of us, here, for in the mid-19th century many shops stayed open until late at night – the markets too at weekends. For entertainment there were numbers of music halls and singing rooms, and numerous beerhouses and dram shops which sold cheap spirits. Between these places of entertainment itinerant salesmen plied their trade, selling such items as sheep's trotters, pig's trotters and hot pies.

SETTING THE SCENE 11

Plan of Bradford at the beginning of the 19th Century.

If we believe contemporary accounts, the streets teemed with life at nights, especially on Fridays and Saturdays. The centre of Bradford and its surroundings did not quieten down until the early hours of the morning. Even then there was abundant evidence of the night's goings on – Burnley again:

> ... people lie about doorways and causeways, so far gone in intoxication as to be quite beyond the power of striking a policeman, or ... going home and beating their hungry wives.

Such behaviour was repugnant to the Victorian middle class who viewed the poorer districts of town and their night life as the breeding grounds for immoralities of all kinds. On reflection, some of this can be put down to a lack of common understanding, the clash between a boisterous working class set on a good time after a long and strenuous working day, and a genteel class who considered themselves the moral arbiters.

Nevertheless, there were serious problems of drunkenness, prostitution and assault, which occasionally flared up into dangerous affrays. In 1844, for instance, a mob of Irishmen had pursued the Idle Prize Band, who had been playing at an Orange Order function, up Otley Road and beat one of its members to death.

The Bradford of the mid-19th century was the result of disorderly social and industrial growth. The increase in the town during the first fifty years of the century went unregulated, and if seamy, overcrowded slums had arisen in some quarters of the town it was largely because there were no laws to control them – houses or factories could be built almost anywhere; there was no proper sewerage system; no pure water supply piped to houses; streets were not drained, many were not paved. Although there was a police force, it was scarcely able to keep order on the streets.

Not until the Borough Council was formed in 1848 was there the beginnings of a modern groundwork of administration, and for several years after that Bradford was to remain a raw and uncouth town. It is among the streets and courts of this older Bradford, in the dark months of November and December 1858 that our story unfolds.

2

The Fatal Events

THE ERROR

Joseph Neal lived in Stone Street tucked away down by the side of the Salem Chapel off Manor Row. Neal was a wholesale confectioner in a small way of business, and his neighbours were similarly placed in life – small shopkeepers, tradesmen and the like. He was on the borders of respectability, comfortably above the working man, but not on a par with the grand folk across the way in Manor Row – solicitors, manufacturers and wool merchants.

He had been born in Halifax, and seems to have come to live in Bradford around 1852, when he was 23. He lived at Stone Street with his wife Patience and they had set up in the business of making sweets. Though a young man he obviously enjoyed a measure of success, for by the later 1850s he employed a number of men in the manufacture of various kinds of sweets. Nothing went to waste. The scrap left over from these, was utilised by throwing them all together in a cheap assortment called Scotch mixtures.

Peppermint lozenges were another of Neal's products. He made them by mixing water, gum, sugar and flavourings to a paste, then spreading it onto boards to dry and cutting it into lozenge shapes. This would normally produce perfectly good sweets. Unfortunately laws about the purity of foods were almost non-existent at this time, and if a cheap alternative were required, then the mixture might be adulterated. The most expensive ingredient was the sugar, and it was a common practice among confectioners to replace part of this with a calcium compound. Opinions differed as to what exactly this was – some said it was plaster of Paris, others ground Derbyshire limestone. It was known euphemistically as terra alba, and colloquially as "daft". Neal was not above sharp practice of this sort himself, but was to protest later, "where I use a pound of it, there are people who will use a ton of it."

All of the sweets, adulterated or otherwise, were made on the premises at Stone Street where Neal lived. His workmen lived in other parts of Bradford, but he did have one lodger, James Archer, who was not employed by Neal, but sometimes fetched ingredients for him. On Monday 18th October, 1858, Archer was going to Baildon, and on his way back he stopped at Shipley at Charles Hodgson's shop, a druggists, where he had agreed to buy a quantity of daft for Neal. Hodgson himself was unwell and his young assistant William Goddard dealt with the order. He had been told by his master that the daft was in a cask in the attic. When he went there, Goddard located the cask, weighed out the white powder into two canvass bags, placed them in a tin box and gave it to Archer. Archer then made his way back to Stone Street, little suspecting that the package which lay beside him in the cart contained not daft, but twelve pounds of arsenic.

THE MIXING

James Appleton was an experienced sweet maker employed by Neal. He was to mix and make the lozenges, common lozenges, that is, adulterated so that they could be sold cheaply. Neal had calculated that about twelve pounds of daft could be added to forty pounds of sugar without attracting attention. The resulting lozenges might then be sold at 8d a pound to retail at between 10d and 12d. It so happened that Neal had received an order for common lozenges from William Hardaker, and this was why the daft had been bought.

Appleton mixed the sugar with the daft and added gum and water, stirring it all into a paste which he smoothed out onto canvass covered boards, and at some point he cut it into lozenges. And there the deadly confection lay for the next ten days or so, slowly hardening until it would be ready for sale.

Both master and assistant should have known something was wrong. Appleton had noticed that the daft appeared smoother, finer and more free flowing than usual. Both men remarked how the mixture and finished product seemed darker than normal. Both had fallen prey to the arsenic — Appleton had sieved the ingredients which caused him to sneeze, and he had then stood bent over the paste as he mixed and worked it together with his hands. He soon became ill and vomited severely. Neal was in the habit of picking up the lozenges occasionally and tasting them for hardness and flavour. He too suffered bouts of vomiting. Yet neither suspected the lozenges. Appleton thought he had taken a chill the day before, while Neal, who had just returned from a trip to Ireland, put it down to a prolonged spell of sea sickness, "having crossed the channel."

THE MARKETING

The Green Market stood on the site of the present day Rawson Market. All trace of it has disappeared, but in 1858 it was a lively place. More than just fruit and vegetables were sold at this market — William Hardaker had his stall there. Hardaker was a "vendor of sweetmeats", to use the parlance of the day, although he was known locally as "Humbug Billy". Aged fifty-

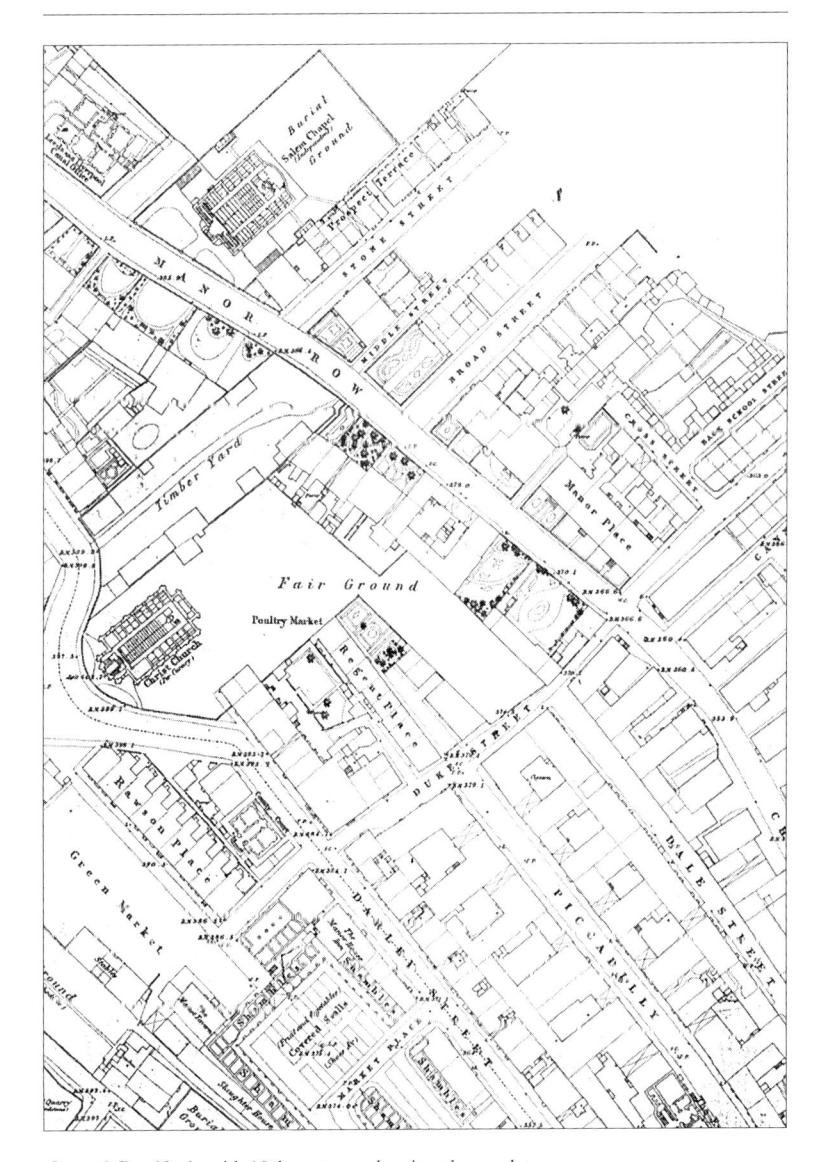

Central Bradford, mid-19th century, showing the markets.

Barkerend from the top of Church Bank. This area has now been cleared, but the engraving conveys well the run-down and smoky character of the place. North Wing, where "Humbug Billy" lived, was situated around here.

five, he had not been selling sweets in this way for more than six or seven years. His original occupation had been a power loom weaver and it was his wife Mary who had been the confectioner. For whatever reason, he had thrown in his lot with hers and had become an established market trader with a nick-name to boot

He had ordered the common lozenges from Neal and it was here that Neal brought them on 30th October. It was a Saturday afternoon and business was brisk. Hardaker examined the lozenges; didn't like the colour much; was unwilling to pay 8d a pound. Neal dropped his price to 7½d; Hardaker agreed and the deal was concluded. "Humbug Billy" was now the owner of forty pounds of poisoned lozenges wrapped up in four ten pound parcels. One of these was opened and went on sale immediately. Unfortunately, Hardaker liked to sample his wares. By half past five he was so ill that he had to be put in a cab and taken home. John Edmondson, his assistant, then took over the stall, selling sweets until eleven thirty that night. In all just over four pounds of the lozenges were sold, mostly in two ounce quantities.

A LESSON ON POISONS

Arsenic is an element which freely forms oxides. Arsenious trioxide, for instance, is a whitish powder which can hardly be tasted when mixed in foodstuffs. It is so poisonous that a mere speck can kill. To be more accurate between three and five grains would be sufficient to kill an adult and there are above four hundred and thirty-seven grains to the ounce. It was discovered by later analysis that each lozenge contained an average of fourteen grains of arsenic, and there were twenty-four lozenges in the two ounce quantities sold – enough to kill the same number of people in theory, although in practice some people might have a far higher tolerance to the poison.

The effects of arsenical poisoning show themselves quickly: terrible pains, intense thirst, gastric and intestinal troubles, blood-stained diarrhoea and vomiting. The victim may linger in this distressing state for several days, or may die within hours after a complete collapse of the circulatory system.

It was such a case that John Henry Bell, a Bradford doctor of Scottish extraction, was called out to treat on the Sunday afternoon of 31st October. Mark Burran, a craftsman who lived off Thornton Road, had bought two ounces of mixed lozenges and pear drops in the Green market on Saturday night. He had eaten some and the next morning his wife Maria had given more to their two young sons. All began to be violently ill. Maria blamed it on the lozenges, but a young man and his wife who lodged with the Burran family poured scorn on this idea and rashly ate some of the lozenges to prove the point. They too were soon writhing and vomiting.

It was about four o'clock in the afternoon when Bell arrived at the Burrans' house in Jowett Street. He examined the children first. Orlando, aged five, was pale; his lips were blanched and livid, his eyes sunk and half closed with a blue line under them and dilated pupils. His pulse was weak. He was, in fact, dying. Quarter of an hour later, he died in Bell's presence. Two-year-old John Henry was in a similar condition, and died about fifteen minutes after his brother.

The death of the boy, the condition of the others and the fact of their all having eaten the lozenges, led Bell to suspect poisoning, arsenic poisoning. He took away with him the last remaining lozenge which he analysed. The result confirmed his suspicions. Later that evening he and his colleague Dr Bronner, who had more of the lozenges, were knocking on the door of Mr Rimmington the analytical chemist. A further test by Rimmington left no room for doubt: the lozenges contained arsenic. It was a police matter now.

MR LEVERATT TAKES CHARGE

The deaths of two other children had been reported to the police at the Swain Street police station on Sunday morning, but it was thought that

Westgate at its junction with Silsbridge Lane. It was in the pubs and dram shops in such districts that Leveratt's officers gave out the dire news.

they had died of cholera, and the deaths were routinely logged down, to be attended to later. By Sunday afternoon further reports of deaths had been coming in, including that of yet another two children who had died in suspicious circumstances. P.C. Campbell was sent to investigate. First he visited the Burrans' household where he found the two dead children. Then, on being told when and from whom the lozenges had been bought, he went round to the house of "Humbug Billy" Hardaker in North Wing. Hardaker was still sick, but told Campbell he had bought the lozenges from Neal. Campbell seized the remaining lozenges – 35lbs 11½ ozs were left from the original 40lbs – and went in pursuit of any left-overs which Neal might have retained.

The news hit Neal like a bombshell. It was possibly the shock of hearing what had happened which made him slow to cooperate at first. "Be quick," Campbell said, "for I want to see my own child." Neal related how he had sold the whole 40lbs to Hardaker except for a few ounces of scrap or waste. This he had thrown in with the Scotch mixtures. The Scotch mixtures were in glasses at Neal's other premises, a shop in the market house on Darley Street, and he and Campbell searched through these until they had extracted about 6ozs of lozenge fragments.

William Burniston, a detective officer, was also on the case. It was probably P.C. Campbell who informed him of the facts, and by eight o'clock that evening, Burniston was at Hodgson the druggists in Shipley with Neal in tow. The two men had a long wait. At ten o'clock, William Goddard the assistant returned home, then, after waiting a further half hour or so in the hope that Hodgson would return also, Burniston asked Goddard to show him where he had found the daft. While Goddard was showing Burniston and Neal the cask in the attic, Hodgson returned. Pointing to the cask, Burniston asked, "Mr Hodgson, what does it contain?" To which Hodgson immediately replied, "Arsenic."

The dire consequences of the situation were now all too clear, and Burniston informed the chief constable, William Leveratt. Leveratt had been appointed chief constable in 1848. An experienced officer who had served his time with the Liverpool police, Leveratt's task was to organise the Bradford force into an efficient and disciplined body of men. The actions he took on that Sunday night certainly show his decisive manner. He had, in fact, been kept informed of events since earlier that evening, and had given orders that the night relief should visit all the beerhouses and inns which were open and warn people not to eat the lozenges, but to hand them in at the police station. He had also sent round two bellmen crying the terrible news until late at night. Now, at well after eleven o'clock, he drew up bills telling of the danger, and had them printed there and then although by this time it was after midnight. These were circulated within a five mile radius of Bradford and by day-break the bills were thickly posted on walls all over the town. Undoubtedly these measures saved lives. But the tragic fact remains that all over Bradford people already lay sick or were dying.

The police continued their enquiries over the next day or so. They were not satisfied with Neal's account of the affair, and, besides, with a potentially fatal epidemic of poisonings about to break out, every fact had to be double checked, every possibility anticipated. As things turned out the police were right to be suspicious, for whether through confusion, or an attempt to preserve some of his merchandise, Neal had not told the complete truth.

When questioned by P.C. Campbell, Neal had insisted that only 6ozs of waste lozenges had been left over. Yet when Shuttleworth, another detective officer, had later searched Neal's premises in Stone Street he had found fragments of hundreds of lozenges adhering to the drying boards. Neal's wife had also admitted to going through yet more portions of Scotch mixtures, removing the lozenges and throwing them on the fire. Shuttleworth twice more returned to Neal's shop in the Market House, and there Neal produced further parcels of Scotch mixtures containing lozenges, which, he said, his wife had taken to the shop unbeknown to

The Market House (sometimes called the old Butter Market) where Neal had a shop. It stood at the entrance to the Green Market which is in the background.

him. But while the key of the shop was being returned to the key holder, Neal "took to his heals and ran off", whereupon Shuttleworth "put a policeman on his track." The foolish man Neal was found sitting in his own kitchen. There was no need for him to run – he was not, as yet, charged with any crime; indeed, he had produced the lozenges from ingredients supplied in good faith. But despondency and alarm had probably induced a fit of panic in him. He had been reported earlier as saying, "I may shut up shop now ... there is an end of it."

COUNTING THE COST

How the public received the news on Monday morning can only be imagined. Newspapers of the day are of some help, but have their limitations. The important local newspaper, the "Bradford Observer", came out only once a week, and so did other newspapers such as the "Leeds Mercury" or "Leeds Intelligencer". The "Times" had reported the event first, but from a distance, and by the time the "Bradford Observer" reported the event on the following Thursday, the paper's publication day, there had already been a number of developments.

"Dreadful Fatality From Poisoning" was the headline to the story. "The excitement and alarm on Monday morning was intense," the report read, "and it has continued to increase from day to day as reports of deaths and

DREADFUL FATALITY FROM POISONING.

SEVENTEEN PERSONS DEAD AND A LARGE NUMBER OF SEVERE SUFFERERS.

THE most dreadful calamity that perhaps ever befel this district has occurred within the last few days. The careless and negligent use of a deadly poison—arsenic—has had the unhappy result already of depriving no fewer than 17 persons of life, and of filling innumerable homes throughout a wide district with suffering, mourning, and woe.

On Sunday morning, two instances of sudden deaths were reported at the Borough Police Station. Two boys—one nine years of age and the other eleven—were reported to have died suddenly. The coincidence, considering the early years of these persons, was certainly an alarming one, duly considered, but, as there was apparently no grounds for suspecting anything unnatural in the incident of these sudden deaths, the fact was duly chronicled in the records of the Police Station, without any grave alarm being excited. As the day wore on, however, the circumstance provoked the fitting suggestion as to the immediate cause which had thus violently stricken down such early boyhood. Sudden deaths were rapidly multiplying on every side, and it was also stated that there

Report in the Bradford Observer, 4th November, 1858.

illness have begun to multiply. The members of the medical profession have never been so busy as they have been these last few days."

Lists of the dead and suffering were posted at the police station. By Wednesday evening there had been seventeen deaths and one hundred and ninety-eight people were ill, some gravely ill. But, as the "Observer" remarked, only deaths needed to be notified, and there were doctors with so many cases of illness to deal with that they had not informed the police of them all. "The list of sufferers published is only an approximation to the extent of the widespread mischief." There were, in fact enough lozenges in circulation to poison between 900 and 1000 people, and they were to turn up in places as far apart as Leeds and Bolton near Manchester. However, the fatalities seem to have been confined to Bradford.

On Saturday November 6th a special edition was printed the "Bradford Observer Extraordinary" giving the latest details. By the following Thursday the "Observer" could report that there had been no further deaths. The final total stood at twenty deaths with perhaps another two or three hundred made seriously ill. Half the dead were children. The rest were of all ages – the youngest 14 years; the oldest 69 years. Arriving at an accurate figure for the seriously ill is difficult. Newspaper reports vary over the years, and, as the "Observer" commented, not all cases had been reported. We should also bear in mind the consequential disorders that the poisoning may have brought on – digestive problems, for instance, which may have troubled some people for years. The grief and affliction this incident caused, then, would have been far more widespread than at first appears. Someone would have to be called to account.

It was among the run-down streets and courts of Bradford that much of the illness due to the poisoning took place – areas such as Silsbridge Lane and Poole Alley, above, which were demolished in the later 19th century.

3

The Prisoner at the Bar

REMANDED

When detective officer Burniston had visited Charles Hodgson's premises at Shipley on that first Sunday of the poisoning, he had arrested Hodgson's assistant William Goddard. It was Goddard who had sold the arsenic, and, at that time, Burniston did not know whether there had been a mistake or whether Goddard had acted maliciously. On Monday morning he was brought before the magistrates at the Court House in Hall Ings. At the hearing, the details of the whole dreadful affair came out. Goddard was remanded in custody. The magistrates met again the following day when they decided that Charles Hodgson ought to be remanded on account of his negligence. On the same day, Tuesday, an inquest was opened by the coroner at the Pack Horse Inn, Westgate. The charge of negligence was again raised, and suspicion was also beginning to fall on Neal – his flight and the confusion over the Scotch mixtures could not have helped. Accordingly, at the hearing on Wednesday morning, Neal too was remanded. After some consultation, it was agreed to remand Goddard and Hodgson in custody, while Neal was to be released on bail.

On Friday, the magistrates felt sufficiently prepared to decide whether the three should stand trial for manslaughter. The hearing was a lengthy one, going on until eleven o'clock that night. The police evidence and the evidence of the other witnesses was restated. But the most striking testimony came from the analytical chemist Felix Rimmington. He had been asked for a thorough analysis of the lozenges. In the ones he had examined he stated that he "had found arsenic in great abundance – in sufficient quantity to destroy life." His methods had been punctilious. In trying to ascertain the amount of arsenic each lozenge contained, he could scarcely believe the first results, they were so high. He therefore began another set of tests, but each time he arrived at similar figures – an average of fourteen grains – "arsenic in great abundance".

He had also been brought the bowels and stomach of a dead child to examine. Again he was to show that arsenic was present in their contents. Dramatically, he held up two glass tubes in court: in one was a portion of the stomach contents of the dead child; in the other the stomach contents of a healthy person. In each he had placed a strip of copper. That belonging to the child clearly showed a deposit of arsenic. Here was compelling forensic evidence.

COURT HOUSE.

The hearing into the poisonings was held by Bradford's magistrates at the Court House shown above. It was built in 1834 on a site in Hall Ings now occupied by the new "Telegraph and Argus" building. Coroners' inquests, however, continued to be held at local inns.

The hearing was resumed on Saturday morning when a decision was reached: the three prisoners were released on bail, but bound over to appear at the York Assizes where they were to stand trial on a charge of manslaughter through negligence. Although they returned home to their own beds, Hodgson, Goddard and Neal could hardly have slept easily. Indeed, Hodgson did not. On the afternoon of the same Saturday an inquest was opened into the deaths of two more people at East Ardsley. The jury found that they had died of arsenic poisoning and thought that Hodgson should be charged with manslaughter. The coroner issued a warrant for his arrest, and on Saturday evening Burniston took Hodgson into custody and conveyed him to the House of Correction at Wakefield.

MR BARON WATSON CONSIDERS

They did not have long to wait, since the assizes were due to be held in December. It would be helpful to know something of the public reaction at this point. Here were three people accused of the manslaughter of a number of adults and children through the adulteration of sweets. Many, many others had been made ill. Yet two were free for the moment; free, indeed, to continue their trade. It would be easy to imagine hostile crowds gathering outside Neal's or Hodgson's premises and their trade in ruins, but the press was silent on these matters. Only one or two reports hint at anything more. When Hodgson was taken to the House of Correction, for example, he did not apply for bail and the "Bradford Observer" commented "... we understand he intends to remain in custody and await the result of his trial" – was this because he was safer in gaol? On the other hand, there seems to have been some sympathy for William Goddard's plight. On November 16th at the Temperance Hall in Leeds Road there was a public lecture on the poisonings and adulteration. While Hodgson was roundly condemned, the speaker giving the vote of thanks suggested that the magistrates had acted wrongly in committing Goddard for trial, "that poor helpless inexperienced boy".

On Tuesday 9th December the Assizes sat at York. They were presided over by Mr Baron Watson and a grand jury was sworn in. In his opening remarks to the jury Baron Watson observed that the case was unusual. To find the charge of manslaughter proved, there was no need in this instance to show a criminal intention on the part of the accused, simply that by their actions they were negligent to the extent that they had caused a death. In which case, he did not see how Neal could be tried at all, since he had not known, and could not have known, that the lozenges contained arsenic, and had not even been present when they were made. Similarly, Goddard had only followed his master's instructions to the best of his abilities. On this advice, the Grand Jury discharged Neal and Goddard. But the charge against Hodgson stood, and he was to be tried later that month.

Christmas Day fell on Saturday in 1858. On Tuesday 21st December, Charles Hodgson stood at the bar in the Court of Assize at York. He was charged with the manslaughter of Elizabeth Mary Midgley of Bradford, a seven year old who had died from eating one of the lozenges. If this charge were proved, other charges of manslaughter would be brought against Hodgson. The prosecution argued "that if a person in carrying on his ordinary business, does so with such carelessness that he is the cause of loss of life he makes himself responsible."

Next came the evidence – the same witnesses, the relation of events which had first had an airing at the Court House in Bradford. Then came William Goddard. He stated his part in the affair much as we have already heard it, but for the first time he revealed, "My master had cautioned me to be careful of the barrel which contained the arsenic, and which he had pointed out to me." Burniston next corroborated the fact that the barrels had no labels, except on their undersides. At this point the judge stopped the trial. He considered that Hodgson "had taken every precaution in showing the boy Goddard which was the arsenic and which the daft cask".

Bermondsey (above) bordered what is now Cheapside, the Midland Hotel and the railway. The area was cleared in the 1880s to make way for extensions to the new Forster Square station and hotel. Elizabeth Mary Midgley lived in the streets in the background of this photograph.

This was, moreover, not a case where the arsenic had been negligently exposed for sale in a retail shop; it was more a sort of a warehouse. He considered, therefore, that there was no case against Hodgson, and directed the jury to bring in a verdict of not guilty. This they did, and Hodgson walked from court a free man in time for Christmas Day.

4

Later Years

DRAMATIS PERSONAE

The discharge of Hodgson by the York Assize Court cannot be thought of as the end of the affair. There were still things to be considered. On a personal level the protagonists must have been scarred by the events. Although found not guilty, they were not exactly innocent, for they had all played some part in the deaths of twenty people and the suffering of hundreds of others. Hodgson in particular was hardly blameless in the careless way he had stored so hazardous a substance as arsenic. He does not appear to have remained in Shipley for long. Judging from his listing in "Jones' Mercantile Directory of Bradford" for 1863, one wonders about his expertise as a chemist or his commitment to the trade for he describes himself as "Chemist and druggist, stuff manufacturer and commission weaver." Shortly after this date he is not heard of again.

Joseph Neal's career seems to have taken a similar course. In 1861, he was still living at Stone Street, but now described himself as a confectioner and *beer seller*. By 1863, he seems to have left the Bradford district.

One person who remained was William Hardaker, "Humbug Billy". Indeed, he was treated in the press with something approaching sympathy, since he had been poisoned himself and lay sick for several days – "disabled by paralysis", as the "Bradford Observer" put it at one point. He went on living at his house in North Wing and continued to sell confectionery from his market stall until about 1870, when he may have died. His son James Hardaker was to continue the family business until the close of the century, when the events of forty years before were already history. "Humbug Billy" came out of the affair surprisingly well, considering he had ordered the adulterated lozenges in the first place.

Initially, the medical profession did not show themselves in a good light. Mark Burran, for example, sick as he was, struggled out on Sunday afternoon seeking medical help – "I went to Mr Roberts and sat me down and waited. I went for Mr Illingworth and he would not come ...". Fortunately, he was able to find John Henry Bell who, as we have seen, realised the seriousness of the situation, and was probably the first to deduce that arsenic was involved. Aged twenty-six at the time, Bell was young and dedicated, and was to become a popular doctor in Bradford where he practised for many years. He died in 1906 while on holiday with his family at Morecambe.

At the time of the poisoning Dr J.H. Bell lived in a house in Westgate. Around 1863 he moved to the above purpose-built house on Lumb Lane with a side entrance on Hallfield Road to his surgery. Bell's initials can be seen today in a medallion on the left hand bay window.

When William Leveratt was appointed Chief Constable of the borough in 1848 his job was to turn the Bradford force into a body of men capable of policing an expanding and disorderly town. His command was certainly tested on this occasion, and the men under his charge did not let him down. Uniformed and detective officers had located the source of the poisoning and detained those involved. Leveratt's lightning action in spreading the word undoubtedly saved lives. Leveratt's force had shown that they could cope with an emergency, and this was recognised by the Watch Committee who rewarded the officers concerned – Leveratt received £5, Burniston £4 while the constables on the inquiry received £2 each. These were not paltry sums, for Burniston's weekly wage was around 30/-, and the top rate constables could earn was about 19/-. Leveratt was not to remain Chief Constable for much longer, and retired through ill-health in 1859, after which date he seems to have left the district.

The other person who behaved with distinction was the chemist Felix Marsh Rimmington. Rimmington was Yorkshire born and had set up his business in Bradford in about 1830. At a time when forensic science was in its infancy he had demonstrated with commendable thoroughness just how relevant such evidence could be.

LATER YEARS 29

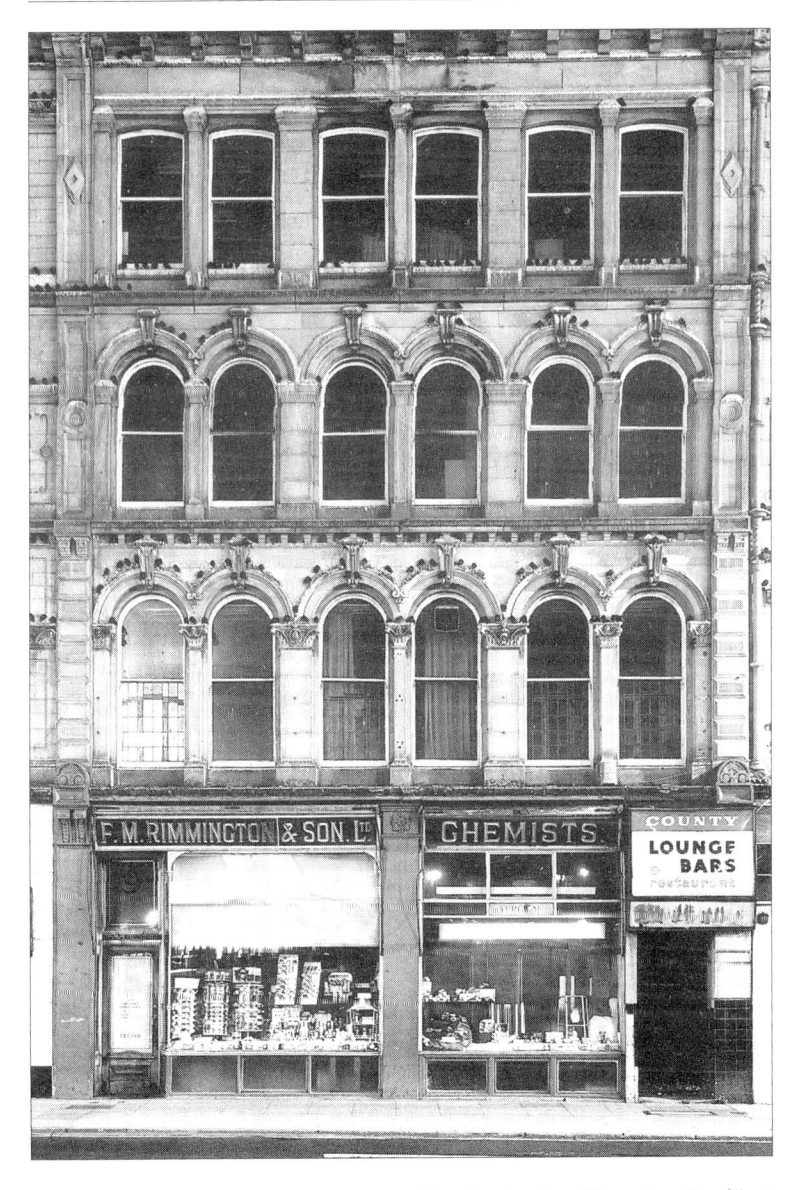

Rimmington's new shop. (*Picture courtesy of Ian Beesley from* Victorian Bradford The Living Past.)

It is fitting that he became the first public analyst to be appointed to the Borough of Bradford. Rimmington also continued working as a chemist in the town, but moved from his original premises in Ivegate into a more commodious shop in Bridge street as the firm of F.M. Rimmington and Son. He died in 1897. The shop survives, although the Rimmington family are no longer connected with it.

IN THE PUBLIC INTEREST

The Bradford poisoning had thrust two issues before the public in a spectacular fashion – the security of poisons and the adulteration of food. Press comment had been concerned as much with these issues as with reporting the events. A correspondent to the "Liverpool Mercury" had written:

> We fear there are plenty of druggists all over England who keep lads in their shops as ignorant as Goddard is said to be, and who allow the most active of poisons to be freely retailed by boys who cannot tell arsenic from plaster of Paris, or oxalic acid from Epsom salts.

and the "Manchester Guardian" commented, "It is now quite certain that chemists and druggists must be prepared for reform"

This perhaps alludes to a bill brought before the House of Commons just before the summer recess of 1858. Since 1852 chemists had been obliged to record all sales of arsenic, but there were no regulations about the storage of poisons. The bill of 1858 aimed to put matters right, but had been introduced late in the session amid opposition from interested parties. Now, in February 1859, the Home Secretary himself introduced a Bill to Regulate the Keeping and Sale of Poisons, for:

> ... all the reasons which urged the propriety of such a Bill last summer are increased, I think, to an amazing extent by the fearful occurrence which took place in the autumn at Bradford.
> [Hansard 8th February, 1859]

But the greatest indignation was reserved for the issue of food adulteration. Concern over this matter had been growing throughout the first half of the 19th century. It was a common practice, as Neal had stated, to use plaster of Paris in confectionery instead of sugar. This sort of thing was not confined to sweets. Brick dust was added to cocoa; sand to sugar; ground acorns to coffee; toxic chemicals as colourings. As early as 1820 the chemist Frederick Accum had published a treatise on adulteration which revealed such practices. Unfortunately, the book enraged food manufacturers to the extent that Accum left the country. In 1850, the "The Lancet" formed an Analytical and Sanitary Committee which analysed samples of food during the years 1851–1854. Again, abundant proof of adulteration was provided. In 1856, the Commons ordered an inquiry and again evidence was presented which showed widespread adulteration. Yet despite all of this evidence, no action was taken.

The Bradford poisoning highlighted the issue at a critical point. "The event ... teaches the folly and wickedness of adulterating articles of food", growled the "Bradford Observer". It was, "a disgrace to our civilisation and Christianity." "Thou shalt not commit adulteration", wrote one correspondent to the "Times", and in the same edition there was a letter from George Moore of Moore and Murphy, a London firm of confectioners:

> Permit me, Sir, as a lozenge manufacturer of more than 40 years standing, to inform you that the adulterating article called duft, duck, stuff, derby, plaster, or by some more classically named terra alba, is used in the manufacture of lozenges to the alarming extent of 25 to 35 per cent ...

After condemning the practice, Moore concluded:

> If the present calamity, awful as it is, and the publicity to the use of terra alba should not be the means of discontinuing it, I trust next session the Legislature will not allow it to pass unnoticed.
> ["The Times", 10th November, 1858]

This was precisely what happened. In February 1859 The Adulteration of Food or Drink Bill received its first reading in the Commons. It was introduced by John Scholefield one of the members for Birmingham. It is a sad reflection on Bradford's M.P.s at this date that they neither sponsored the Bill nor spoke in the debates. They were Titus Salt and Henry Wickham.

The Bradford affair was to surface again, however. On the second reading the Conservative member for Leominster, Gathorne Hardy, moved that the Bill be postponed. Such legislation needed thinking about more carefully, since it would create a system "of informing and spying in respect of articles of food sold in this country"; it treated "the people of this country like children" and lead them "to depend upon Parliament instead of themselves". Hardy was Bradford born, and had become M.P. for Leominster in the 1850s, after he had been rejected as the Conservative candidate for Bradford in the 1847 election. He had, however, kept up his Bradford connections, and it was probably this that brought the retort from Lord Robert Cecil "[Has my] hon. Friend forgotten the Bradford poisoning case?" Hardy's motion to adjourn the reading was dismissed. After this the Bill received an easy passage through both Houses, and received the Royal Assent in August 1860.

The new Act empowered magistrates to impose fines for selling adulterated food or drink, and enabled local authorities to appoint public analysts to assist them in this work. This was only the first in a series of acts concerned with the quality of food and public safety. If anything good had come out of the dreadful poisoning in Bradford, it was its effect in speeding along legislation such as this which was much needed in the mid-19th century.

A NOTE ON SOURCES

The text is based almost entirely on newspaper reports of the day. The "Times", "Manchester Guardian" and "Liverpool Mercury" all carry reports and correspondence. The best and most thorough source, however, is the "Bradford Observer" for November and December 1858.